This book is lovingly dedicated to anyone who has ever known what it is to love a pet as a member of their own family, and to my faithful forever pets Sammy and Oliver. **John Graziano**

PUBLISHING

Publishing Director Anne Marshall
Editorial Director Becky Miles
Art Director Sam South
Senior Designer Michelle Foster
Assistant Editor Charlotte Howell
Design Ark Creative
Reprographics Juice Creative

Published by Scholastic Inc. SCHOLASTIC and associated logos are trademarks and/or
registered trademarks of Scholastic Inc,, 557 Broadway, New York , NY 10012

ISBN 978-0-545-38077-5

12 11 10 9 8 7 6 5 4 3 2 1   12 13 14 15 16 17/0
Printed in the U.S.A.   40
First printing, January 2012

PUBLISHER'S NOTE
While every effort has been made to verify the accuracy of the entries in this book,
the Publisher cannot be held responsible for any errors contained in the work.
They would be glad to receive any information from readers.

WARNING
Some of the stunts and activities in this book are undertaken by experts and should
not be attempted by anyone without adequate training and supervision.

INTRODUCING...
JOHN GRAZIANO

John, Ripley's very own cartoonist, has drawn every cartoon in this wacky book of crazy pet stories.

A new Ripley's cartoon has been produced every day for the past 90 years by a dedicated Ripley's cartoonist. John is only the eighth person to take on this role. Amazingly, he got himself the job 25 years after sending his drawings to Ripley's as a teenager!

SPEEDY QUESTIONS!

1. Q: What tools do you use for your drawings?
A: My actual drawings are done the old-fashioned way with pencil, pen and ink, and brush and ink to paper. For airbrushing and coloring I use a Wacom digital tablet.

2. Q: If you hadn't become an artist what would you be?
A: I actually wanted to be a paleontologist and dig up fossils! I do that as a hobby though.

3. Q: Have your pets ever done anything silly?
A: Every day! Lately, my dogs Simon and Spidey have been stealing my socks at a rate of at least one pair a day.

4. Q: What is the most unusual pet you have ever seen?
A: I've heard that people keep jellyfish!

HOW TO DRAW...
SIMON THE DOG

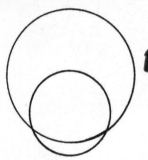

1. Simon is my little pal. He's a tiny terrier who gets into big mischief! To draw him, start with a large and a small circle overlapping each other.

2. Draw two small circles resting on top of the inner circle, and then erase the inner circle.

3. Draw a downward pointing triangle on each side of the outer circle, and then erase the circle lines inside the triangles. Draw an oval at the bottom of the circle.

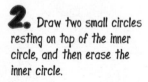

4. Add two lines at the bottom to form the start of the neck, and color in Simon's eyes and nose. He is beginning to come to life!

5. Simon is shaggy-haired so replace the straight lines with wiggly ones. Also, add a little mouth shape under the nose.

6. Give Simon some whiskers and hair lines. Add a collar and a round dog tag. Put some shading in the fur and add the little white dots on the eyes. Erase a bit of the tip of the nose to give it a wet look. Watch out! Simon is ready for trouble!

Go to www.ripleybooks.com for more amazing facts

WOOF!

Pets

You won't believe the crazy things pets get up to when you look inside this fun-packed book! Meet Nora the piano-playing cat, Harvey the trampolining terrier, Twiggy the water-skiing squirrel, and many more!

It's Ripley's Shout Outs!

Pet-eating python

A snake with a large bump in its tummy attracted attention
in Columbus, Ohio, in 2002. The police were called
to look under a house where the

10-FOOT-LONG PYTHON

had been spotted. Neighbors whose dog was missing feared the
worst—and, sure enough, the bulge in the snake's belly sadly
turned out to be their beloved pet.

What a job!
Edwin Rose of
Hayes, England, is a
professional dog- and
cat-food taster.

Turtle-y illegal

An elderly Chinese man was so determined to travel with his pet
turtle that he tried to smuggle it onto his flight to Chongqing.
The man fastened the turtle, which measured 8 inches across
its shell, onto his back under his clothes, pretending to be a
hunchback. He made it past security, but a guard stopped him
from boarding because his hump didn't look right.

PAW-FECT MANNERS

Faye Murrell felt lonely with no one to share mealtimes...

...so she taught Tessa, her cat, how to hold a fork. Now the clever cat...

...eats at the dinner table and has also learned how to use chopsticks if noodles are on the menu.

She is also allowed to eat ice cream on special occasions, which she eats with a spoon!

PERFORMING PET

Jaroslav Kana from the Czech Republic is grooming his pet to be the "mane" attraction in TV shows and ads: He's the proud owner of Leon the lion! Jaroslav bought Leon from a private breeder, and can often be seen out walking with the big cat.

Improper parrot

In 1996, a parrot was reported to the Canadian government's French language monitoring office. The parrot was on sale at a pet shop in Napierville, Quebec, but only spoke English, not French, which is the official language of Quebec.

Sebastian the cat has gold crowns, worth $1,900, on his two bottom canine teeth. His owner is David Steele, a dentist from Alexandria, Indiana, who did the dental work himself.

My dog can read!

Willow the terrier can really read! Her owner, animal trainer Lyssa Rosenberg from New York, has taught Willow to recognize written instructions. Show her the words

and she sits on her back legs to beg;

makes her play dead, and "wave" brings a cheery paw in the air to greet you. She knows 250 other tricks, and took just six weeks to learn how to read.

BLOWN AWAY

A tiny Chihuahua was blown over a mile through the
air by a huge gust of wind! Tinker Bell, who only

WEIGHS 6 POUNDS,

was standing on her owner's platform trailer at a
flea market in Waterford Township, Michigan,
when the sudden blast of air sucked her up
and threw her out of sight at

70 MILES PER HOUR!

Luckily, she was found, unhurt
but all shook up!

Napoleon the cat, owned by Fanny Shields of Baltimore, Maryland, was so good at predicting the weather that newspapers would contact her for their forecasts!

Fish out of water

Sparkle the goldfish is one fortunate fish: He survived

7 HOURS OUT OF HIS TANK

before being rescued and returned to the water. It seems he jumped right out and landed behind the tank stand at his home in North Yorkshire, England. He was found, covered in fluff, but appeared to be fine after a quick wash under the kitchen tap. Remember: Look before you leap!

AWESOME ANIMALS...

Millionaire moggy

Linda McManamon of Galveston, Texas, claims that her cat picked her lucky lottery numbers when she won $3,700,000!

LUCKY!

Helping paw

Dogs are famous for lending a helping paw—fetching slippers and newspapers for their owners. A retriever called J.C. from Penn Hills, Pennsylvania, goes the extra mile to help, by collecting prescriptions from the local drugstore for his owners Chuck and Betty Pusateri.

A mutant piglet, born in 2007 at a Chinese farm, had two faces on its supersized head. It had two mouths but only three eyes.

This little piggy

Arne Braut, a pig farmer from Norway, has come up with an unusual way to keep his pigs happy and under control. He pretends he's a pig, too! He wears a pig mask and grunts at his herd to get up close and pig-sonal.

SAY WHAT?

A Red Tibetan Mastiff called Big Splash was once sold in China for the unbelievable sum of $1.5 million.

Wordy bird
Camille Jordan's pet parrot, Puck, of Petaluma, California, could say over 1,700 words!

Cat rescue
Gary Rosheisen owes a lot to his clever cat, Tommy. He trained his pet to dial 911, so when an emergency arose, Tommy could come to the rescue. Sure enough, the training paid off in 2005 when Gary, from Columbus, Ohio, fell from his wheelchair. Tommy successfully dialed the emergency services and saved the day.

Mind-reading dog
Bozo the dog was anything but a bozo—he could read minds! He found fame at the State Fair of Texas in 1938. His master, Captain E.C. Lower, would think of a number, and Bozo would bark it out. He could also bark the number of rings hidden on audience members' fingers, or the denomination of coins hidden in their hands.

COOL FOR CATS

Cats love to scratch, climb, run, and snooze in the sun—so Frances Mooney and Bob Walker have created a cat paradise in their home in San Diego, California. It started with a 9-foot scratching pole, covered with 400 feet of rope. Now they've spent around $10,000 to add 140 feet of overhead walkways and cat-sized stairs.

They also built some sunshine ledges, cutouts to let the cats run from room to room, and even a cats-only clubhouse!

LOOKY-LIKEYS

Roll up, roll up, and join the Key West Fantasy Fest. The ten-day event, held in Florida each year, includes a

PET MASQUERADE AND PARADE

where pets and their owners dress up in matching outfits. Entrants include Todd Heins in reptile makeup with his green iguana, several superheroes and superdogs, and Peri Stone and Woody, who dressed in the Beatles' *Yellow Submarine* costumes together.

Hunter York from Centertown, Kentucky, has a two-headed snake as a pet! He found the king snake in his backyard and kept it, calling it Mary-Kate and Ashley.

A dog's life

Dog lovers can now book a room for their dogs in a luxury canine hotel in France. Actuel Dogs charges around $40 a night, and canine guests can take a swim in the pool, have a dog massage, go jogging, or retire to their room to watch a DVD.

DOUBLE RESCUE

A pet cockatoo named Geronimo escaped from his cage and chose to perch up a pine tree in Montgomery County, Texas. Major problems arose when his owner, William Hart, climbed 60 feet up to reach the bird, and then got stuck, too. He had to be rescued by a coast guard helicopter!

Poor Bubba, a dog from Poole, England, swallowed a rubber duck and had to have it surgically removed.

BOUNCING BULL TERRIER

A Staffordshire bull terrier called Harvey used a child's trampoline to bounce out of his owner's garden in York, England.

HARVEY MADE HIS ESCAPE

in June 2008 by bouncing right over the fence into his neighbor's yard. After four days, he was found and returned to his home.

Cat chat

A hand-held console called the "Meowlingual" helps people understand what their cats are saying! Launched in 2003 by a Japanese toy company, the machine records a cat's meows and purrs and compares them to thousands in its memory. It then translates them into an emotion, such as happy, sad, frustrated, or hungry, with a cute cat face on the screen showing how it's feeling, too.

Ripley's HOME FROM HOME

The Cummins family moved and sadly lost their pet hamster in the process.

A few years later, they were on the move again. Still no sighting of their hamster.

Roberto, a Dutch rabbit, was so big he slept on a dog's bed instead of squeezing into a hutch. In 2004 he measured nearly 4 feet long and weighed 47 pounds!

Doggy paddle

Henry the retriever had a lucky escape after he chased a seagull and plummeted right off the edge of a cliff. His owner, Louise Chavannes, watched in horror at Beachy Head in England, certain that Henry would be killed. He broke one of his legs, but the ocean softened his fall and he swam bravely back to shore to be rescued.

Hey, hammy! It turned out that when the Cummins moved, so did their pet! Using the sofa as a nest...

...their hamster had been sneaking out at night to feed from their other pets' bowls.

Crafty cat

Mary Martell packed her bags and checked in at an airport in New Brunswick, and then boarded her two-hour flight to Ontario, Canada. Imagine how surprised she was when she unpacked in her hotel room, and her cat Ginger

JUMPED OUT

of the suitcase! Ginger had stowed away, and wasn't even spotted by airport security.

President Calvin Coolidge kept Rebecca, his pet raccoon, at the White House, and loved to laugh at guests who were shocked at the sight of her.

Puppy love

Dogs in love can rent a hotel room to spend time alone together! The special

DOGS-ONLY MOTEL

is in Sao Paulo, Brazil, and costs 100 reals ($54) for two hours. It is furnished with a bone-shaped headboard on the bed, paw-print patterns, and heart-shaped mirrors. It even has doggy-controls to dim the lights and play romantic music or movies.

SURPRISING SOUNDS

What would you think if you heard roaring noises coming from an apartment near yours? Neighbors of Antoine Yates heard exactly that and were shocked to find out the cause: He was keeping a 400-pound tiger in his tiny fifth-floor Manhattan apartment. Not only that, he also had a 5-foot-long alligator. He says he was trying to create his own Garden of Eden!

PUSSYCAT F.M.

Does your cat love to dance? Then tune in to Cat Galaxy, an online radio station run by cats, for cats! The station manager, assistant, and program director are all felines, and approve the playlists for programs such as Purr Party, Meow Mixing, and Feline Frenzy. It's all the brainchild of Nohl Rosen of Scottsdale, Arizona, and his cat, Isis.

Ripley's—**Believe It or Not!**®

A German shepherd dog that was often taken for walks along a golf course had surgery to remove 28 golf balls from its stomach.

Aquatic ape

Super swimmer Suryia is unusual in the orangutan world. Usually, these great apes don't like water, but trainers at Myrtle Beach Safari, South Carolina, noticed how much Suryia loved

SPLASHING AROUND

in the bath. They decided to try him in the pool, and he took to it like... erm... a duck to water. Now he swims every sunny day, diving in on the back of his trainer and then splashing off on his own using a very basic "Borneo crawl."

Robert Garnett surprises visitors to Manningtree, England, when he takes his pet iguana for daily walks.

CLEVER CRITTERS...

Water wings
Dogs who can't doggy paddle can still stay safe in the water, using the Float-a-Pet. The device looks like a collar, but if your pet pooch falls overboard, slips on the poolside, or gets swept away in a flood, sensors are activated which inflate the collar and keep your dog's head above water until help is available.

WOW!

Scaredy cat
Chad Russell's tiny but brave Jack Russell terrier chased a mountain lion up a tree in South Dakota in 2010!

A rescue dog named Rhoadi flew 6 feet in the air as part of the Highest Jumper competition in New York's 2002 Greatest American Mutt Show!

Purr-pardon?
Eyup Mrtluturk, living in the Turkish town of Konya, owned a talking cat! The man thinks his pet, Pala, was jealous when people paid more attention to his grandchildren, so the black-and-white tomcat began to talk in Turkish, like a baby.

AMAZING!

Coolidge's critters

President Calvin Coolidge was famous for the animals he kept while at the White House. Along with dogs, cats, birds, and raccoons, he also had a bobcat called Smokey, a pygmy hippo called Billy, a donkey, a wallaby, a bear, and lion cubs given to him as a gift!

INCREDIBLE!

Three French biologists studying fleas living on pets have discovered that dog fleas jump higher than cat fleas!

Time please

A Jack Russell terrier owned by a pub landlord in Bristol, England, became famous for ringing the bell to tell customers it was time to go home.

AWESOME!

Foxy friend

Mike Towler from Tunbridge Wells, England, keeps cats as pets. Nothing unusual there—except the cats are kept company by a friendly fox called Cropper. The poor animal suffers from a memory-damaging disease that makes it dangerous for him to live alone in the wild, so Mike gradually tamed him. Now Cropper eats from a dog bowl and curls up indoors with his cat-friends.

FULL HOUSE

If your parents say your house is too small to keep pets, point them in the direction of Riana van Nieuwenhuizen from Bloemfontein, South Africa. She finds room to keep three dogs, two wolves, three leopards, nine cheetahs, plus a lion and a jaguar! They were all rescued and hand-reared by Riana, who lets them share her kitchen and even her bed.

Poodle-loo

A French poodle named Pierre Deux has his own private bathroom, complete with custom decorations. His owner, Ilia Macdonald, splashed out $795 for a painting that shows Pierre's girlfriend, Gigi, and a note "written" by Pierre saying he'd taken her to Paris. His toilet is decorated with a purple feather boa and aqua chiffon, although he does his doggy-doos on disposable diapers scattered around the floor.

DANCING DOG

Step back from the dance floor and let Samson take center stage: He's the amazing disco dancing dog! The border collie from Manchester, England, loves to

SPIN, TWIRL, AND JUMP

in time to his favorite tunes, and can stand on his back legs to do a pet-perfect version of Michael Jackson's moonwalk.

Sheep pig

A Kune Kune pig from Herefordshire, England is being trained like a dog! His owner, Wendy Scudamore, calls him Sue (after the song "A Boy Named Sue") and has already taught him to

SHAKE HANDS

—or trotters. Sue started copying farm dogs doing agility tests when he realized they got treats for their tricks. Wendy is sure Sue is clever enough to herd sheep, just like the pig in the movie *Babe*.

Pie, a cross-breed dog from Oxfordshire, England, was so addicted to eating grass that surgeons found a pound of it in his stomach. His weight was three times what it should have been because he couldn't digest so much green stuff.

DOGGIE DANCING

It's the craze that's sweeping the nation: Canine freestyle is a form of dog handling and discipline set to music. Pets learn to weave and move in time to the music. Many dogs are so good at it they can throw in a few leaps and spins, too. Other popular show-stoppers include paw kicks, backward moves, and begging or "play dead" tricks.

O2 4 K9S

A human therapy known as OWND (oxygen, water, nutrition, detox) is now available for people and their pets, too. The OWND café in Tokyo, Japan, has 12

CANINE O_2 CAPSULES

for small, medium, or large dogs to inhale pure oxygen and enjoy rejuvenation. Then they can eat a nutritious snack alongside their owners.

A PRINCESS FOR DINNER

Princess the horse is royalty in her own way. Her owner, Carissa Boulden from Sydney, Australia, lets her pet pony eat from the family dining table. Princess can munch through a plate of spaghetti, no problem. She is even allowed to drink beer on Sundays!

IN THE DOG HOUSE

This isn't a kennel like you've seen before. Pampered pooches Chelsea, Darla, and Coco Puff have their own Victorian-style mini mansion that cost their owner $20,000. Tammy Kassis, who lives on the outskirts of Los Angeles, has provided her pets with an 11-foot-tall house that has heating and air conditioning, fancy wallpaper, handmade curtains, TV, and a lawn with a picket fence.

A Persian cat named Sugar walked 1,500 miles in 14 months! Despite having a bad hip, Sugar hiked from Anderson, California, to Gage, Oklahoma to rejoin its owners after they moved out of their house.

CHOMP

CHOMP

PARROT POOP

Owning a pet bird can be a messy business—flying free, the birds are well-known for leaving their mark on furniture when nature calls. Well, Mark and Lorraine Moore have come to the rescue with

BIRD DIAPERS!

Their U.S. business sells Lycra suits with changeable panty pads in all sorts of sizes, colors, and designs, so your feathered friend can be a dedicated follower of fashion without making a mess!

ARE YOU HAVING A LAUGH?

Having a pet hyena sounds like no laughing matter—yet Faten Shwaykani and her son keep hyenas at home.

They let the hyenas roam free in their Syrian house, where the two pets eat eggs for breakfast in the kitchen.

The unusual pets also bathe in the family bathroom...

...and lounge around watching TV when they're feeling lazy!

TUNER FISH

Jor Jor is a goldfish with a fine ear for music! She has been trained by her owner, Diane Rains from Wisconsin, to play the hand bells by pulling strings with her mouth. The wet pet loves to play along to Barbra Streisand songs and especially likes the notes F and D. Jor Jor has even played on national TV, on the show *American Idol*.

CAT AND MOUSE

It's just like a scene from *Tom and Jerry*: Poor Mindy the cat tried to catch a field mouse hiding in a jelly jar, and ended up getting her head totally stuck. Mindy was rescued from the roadside in Peterborough, England, trying to grab the mouse that was just beyond reach at the end of the jar. Eventually, Mindy escaped by smashing the jar on the floor— and the mouse scurried to safety.

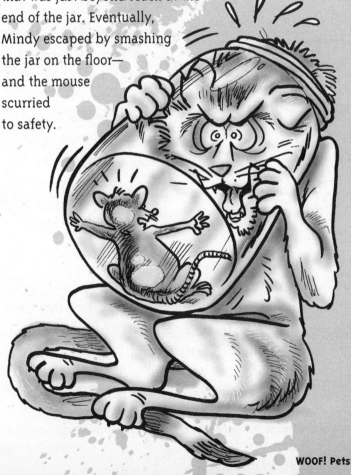

CRAZY CREATURES...

Meow meow

In 2008, a two-faced kitten was born in Perth, Australia. It had two noses, four eyes, and could meow from its two mouths at the same time.

AMAZING!

Knowing he shouldn't be bringing a tortoise into England, a student tried to smuggle it into the country inside his sock!

INCREDIBLE!

Pricey flight

A four-hour flight cost $32,000 because an Israeli woman hired a whole compartment for her boxer dog Orchuk. The dog traveled business class on an El Al flight from Paris, France, to Tel Aviv, and the airline even had to take out some seats to fit the dog's cage on the plane.

Tortoise in the trash

A pet tortoise from Kent, England, survived the trauma of being thrown in the trash by mistake! The shell-shocked pet was taken away in a garbage truck, nearly scooped up by a bulldozer, and saved just before he was headed for the crusher at the local recycling plant.

Look no hands

A mongrel pup born without front legs has learned to walk upright like a human! Faith, from Oklahoma City, can even chase cats on her two back legs.

Pets in uniform

What would your dog look like in the Marines? Or your cat if it joined the army? Now you don't even have to imagine: A website called "Pets in Uniform" will send you a picture! All you do is upload a pic of your pet, and they will send you a photo of it dressed in the uniform of your choice. Company... march!

Parsnip, a basset hound from Shropshire, England, chews anything and everything. In 2007, veterinarians removed a pair of pantyhose from his insides!

High flyers

Carpenter John Looser from Toronto, Canada, can create the ultimate bird house for your feathered friends. His mighty mansions are up to 81 square feet, and can cost $2,500. The most luxurious houses have over 100 rooms and a birdy swimming pool!

AWESOME!

I DO

Two pet pigs oinked "I do" at their own marriage ceremony in Taiwan in 2007. The male pig, Xu Fuge, was being rewarded for his hard work on the farm of Xu Wenchuan, who found him a porky bride to say thank you. The proud piggies were blessed by a priest, and had parrots as their bridesmaid and groomsman.

Ripley's—**Believe It or Not!®**

Fish kiss

Chino, a golden retriever, has a strange love in his life: a fish called Falstaff! His owner, Dan Heath of Medford, Oregon, wondered what his dog was doing when he leaned over the fishpond each day. Chino watches and waits until the carp pops his face out of the water and then the two gently touch noses. Awww!

The Russian blue breed of cat often has an extra toe on one or all of its paws.

Best seller

A clever dog named Hello goes shopping by herself, and serves customers in her owners' store! Visitors to the nut store in Pingdong City, Taiwan, watch in wonder as Hello

OPENS THE REFRIGERATOR,

picks out the nuts, puts them on the counter, and takes the money. When it's grocery time, she waits in line, then hands over money and a shopping list before trotting home with the goods.

RIPLEY'S BRIGHT SPARK

Mo Zhaoguang of the Hubei province of China was getting really mad at his wife. For five years he had blamed her for leaving a light on in their barn overnight. To settle the matter, he slept in the barn.

That very night he discovered that the real culprit was their buffalo who lived in the barn and had learned to pull the light cord with its mouth.

The buffalo would switch on the light to eat or drink, and then turn it off again to sleep!

IT LOOKS LIKE REINDEER

Dobbey is a slightly unusual pet: He's a reindeer!
His owner, Gordon Elliott, takes him for walks around
London, and Dobbey even rides on the local trains
over the festive season to give fellow passengers
something to talk about.

BOW-WOW BEACH

Dogs are banned from most Italian beaches, so your favorite pet has to stay home while you have fun in the sun and surf. However, on Bau Beach, just north of Italy's capital Rome, it's a different story. This beach charges 5 euros ($7) per pooch, and gives them a dog bowl, a towel, an umbrella, and a high-pressure hose down to get rid of any sand between their claws. It's all super-clean, too: The owners are given a pooper scooper to use when nature calls!

Hollywood's first dog star was a German shepherd called Rin Tin Tin. His canine career included making

27 MOVIES

and various radio shows, and he has been honored with a star on the Hollywood Walk of Fame at 1623 Vine St. He signed his contracts with a paw print, and when he died in 1932 it was front-page news.

DO YOU SERVE CROCODILES?

They did at a bar in Noonamah, Australia, in 2008! A 2-foot-long croc made its way into the human watering hole, so the regulars gave it a beer and then seized the opportunity to tape up its jaws before taking it to a wildlife center.

Tom K. Maunupau from Honolulu, Hawaii, had a pet shark and took rides on its back!

PERFORMING POODLE

Chanda-Leah is one clever canine. She toured North America with her owner, Sharon Robinson, performing over 1,000 tricks. The perfect poodle, from Ontario, Canada, has also appeared on TV, and can do all kinds of things, from untying shoelaces to playing the piano. She's also potty trained, knows how to skateboard, and can sort out junk mail and throw it away!

Wrong turn

Racing-pigeon fanatic John Elsworth of Houston, Texas, thought it would be a good idea to ask his girlfriend

TO MARRY HIM

by sending a note with one of his birds. Unfortunately for his girlfriend, the pigeon got lost and delivered the proposal to another woman, Rita Williams. Believe it or not, Rita and John then met, fell in love, and got married!

MUSIC BY MEOW-ZART?

Nora is a tabby with a talent: She can play the piano with her paws! Adopted by music teacher Betsy Alexander, in Philadelphia, Pennsylvania, Nora used to watch the piano lessons with interest. One day she leaped onto the piano stool and started to play! Now she even has her own CD, DVD, downloadable ringtone, and over ten million hits on the Internet from people watching her pick out a tune.

FALSE ALARM

Marjorie Johnson's dog wiped the smile off her face in 2007 when he swallowed her false teeth! The Jack Russell terrier, named Desmond, downed her dentures one morning, and had to be taken for emergency surgery to get them back. Desmond isn't the only dog with a taste for teeth: The same thing has happened with Bramble, a collie-cross in England, and T'Pol, a dachshund in Denver, Colorado.

SLOW BUT FAITHFUL

Yang Jinsen from Dongwan in China has a pet snail that has stayed by his side since 1997! He found the snail by the roadside on his way home from school and loves it so much that he plays with it and takes it for walks. He's also built it a home, and in 2007 introduced it to the woman he wanted to marry. The tender loving care has paid off as the snail has lived twice as long as snails normally do.

SILLY SNAKE

Now this is a tricky situation: Reggie the king snake
had to have surgery because he tried to eat his own tail!
The 3-foot-long king snake thought its own tail was a
tasty meal, but one bite told him how wrong he was.
Unfortunately, his backward-facing teeth stopped him from
spitting it out, and veterinarian Bob Reynolds from England
had to dislocate the snake's jaw to pull out the tail.

Suang Puangsri shares his home in Thailand with an extraordinary number of pet scorpions, about 4,600 in total! He performs his daily Buddhist meditations surrounded by the super-stingers, and has been stung so often that he says he now believes himself to be immune to their venom.

Pet pigs

People with allergies are going crazy for the latest designer pet: a hairless guinea pig. These

"SKINNY PIGS"

were created decades ago in research labs where their fur-free coat was used to test skin treatments. Now they are so popular that pet-owners will pay up to $250 for one. They are high-maintenance, though, as they need to be kept warm in winter and have sun protection applied in the summer.

Delores Whittington's cat has five toes on each paw and two tongues.

CRITTER KINGDOM

In loving memory

Goran and Karmen Tomasic were so upset when their Dalmatian, Bingo, was run over that they painted their house in Pribislavec, Croatia, white with black spots in his memory.

WOW!

Fire hazard

Peggy, a Rottweiler puppy from Northumberland, England, set her home on fire when she tried to reach a chocolate cake in the kitchen and accidentally switched on the stove. Clever Peggy survived the flames and smoke by jumping into the bathtub and breathing air through the plughole.

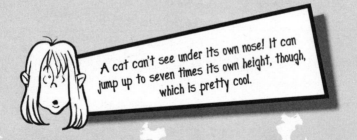

A cat can't see under its own nose! It can jump up to seven times its own height, though, which is pretty cool.

Safe sticks

Now you don't have to worry about your dog swallowing splinters. You can buy a rubber stick, called SafeStix, for your pet to play with.

AMAZING!

Snake walking

Walking a pet snake on a leash through public parks is now illegal in Osnago, Italy. It had become such a trendy thing to do that the mayor had to ban it for safety reasons.

INCREDIBLE!

X-ray pets

Imagine how surprised customs officers were at Dublin Airport, Ireland, when their X-ray scanner showed a dog packed in a bag! When it appeared on their screen it was standing so still that officers thought it was a toy dog at first. The tiny Chihuahua had been smuggled from Spain inside a traveler's hand luggage, and was unharmed by the journey.

The Leroy family from Washington were shocked to find out that a stray dog was sleeping in their car at night—it could open the door by itself!

Look into my eye

Check out Peavey the horse's unbelievable eyeball: Peavey, who belongs to Ann Huth-Fretz of Tiffin, Ohio, has a two-tone eye, with the colors split right down the center.

Mane attraction

A horse from California made the headlines with its amazing mane—measuring 14 feet long—and its 13-foot-long tail.

AWESOME!

Lobster dogs

Yes, you read that right: lobster dogs! Dogs
dressed up as lobsters, in fact. It's all part of
the annual Los Angeles Lobster Festival, a food
and music weekend that features a

DOG FANCY DRESS PARADE!

Owners dress their dogs as a variety of seafood- and
general ocean-based items, from sushi and
fishcakes to seals, whales, and starfish.
It has to be seen to be believed...

Red, a lurcher living at Battersea Dogs
Home, London, was no dumb hound.

Every day, Red used his nose and teeth
to unlock and relock his door—and let
out, and lock in, his friends, too.

Aping around

Have you ever seen an orangutan on a jet ski? You can if you go to The Institute of Greatly Endangered and Rare Species (TIGER) in Miami, Florida. Their four-year-old orangutan, Surya, puts on his wetsuit and jets around for all to see. He wears a life jacket to keep him afloat, though, as he doesn't like getting his head wet.

Du Hebing, a shepherd from Xi'an City, China, couldn't afford a new sheepdog when his died, so instead he herded his sheep himself by using a picture of a wolf.

WOAH!

Alexandre Dumas, the French author, had a pet vulture, and took it for walks on a leash!

For days, staff arrived to find chaos in the kitchen. They had to install security cameras to figure out who was to blame!

DOG HANDLER

In Sydney, Australia, in May 2005, Andrew Larkey successfully walked 11 dogs at the same time. He started the walk trying to keep 19 dogs under control, but after being pulled in too many directions, he finally walked 2/3 mile with 11 dogs all headed (roughly) the same way.

Hamster power

Peter Ash has harnessed hamster power! The 16-year-old from Somerset, England, invented a device that hooks up his cell phone to the exercise wheel of his hamster Elvis. When

ELVIS SPINS THE WHEEL

it charges the phone, and Peter gets about 30 minutes of talk time for every two minutes his hamster runs.

CRAZY CANINES

The Great American Mutt Show takes place every year around the U.S.A. Instead of the usual events, you can put your pet up for trophies such as Best Kisser, Best Lap Dog Over 50 Pounds, Waggiest Tail, Looks Most Like Another Animal, and, for those ugly pugs, the "Face Only A Mother Could Love" award.

GREAT AMERICAN MUTT SHOW

CHILLY CHUCKS

Four hens that were saved from life at a factory farm have inspired a new fashion in the feathered world. The "chux tux" is a knitted jacket, designed by Brigitte Hawley from Kent, England, to keep chickens warm. It covers the parts that have been pecked free of feathers during life in the crowded shed, but leaves the hens' wings free so they don't lose their balance.

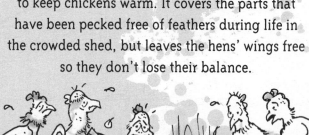

RIPLEY's LIFE SAVER

1.

In 2007, Debbie Parkhurst saw her life flash before her eyes as she choked on a piece of apple.

2.

Toby to the rescue! Debbie's dog knew just what to do!

3.

In the style of the Heimlich Maneuver, Toby dislodged the apple by jumping on Debbie's chest.

4.

As soon as Debbie began to breathe again, Toby licked her back to liveliness!

The Jouberts have not one, but TWO hippos who call their house a home! The first, Jessica, was washed up in floods in 2000 when she was just a baby. Tonie Joubert, a game warden, knew how to care for her, and Jessica was soon part of the family. She even slept in her own double bed at their home in Mozambique! Now she's too big for that, and sleeps on the patio, where she has been joined by Fred, another hippo who loves the Jouberts' company too much to leave.

COOL FOR DOGS

Dog owners who care for their canines' eyes (and want them to look cool in the sunshine) have been snapping up sunglasses made for their dogs. Several Internet companies sell the shades in sizes to suit the biggest bruisers to the smallest lap dogs. Check out Doggles in the U.S.A. or Germany's Dog-Goes in Munich for accessories to protect your pet in the glare of the sun.

Dogs don't drive

It was pure car crash TV for anyone watching as Li, a lady from Hohhot in China, attempted to give her dog a

DRIVING LESSON.

She said that the dog loved to crouch on the steering wheel while she drove, so she thought she'd try letting it steer while she operated the foot pedals. Not surprisingly, the team crashed their car...

HELLO KITTY!

When the Honer family cat, Louis, went missing for four weeks, they thought a coyote had taken him. That's until Mr. Honer opened the refrigerator in their barn, and out fell poor Louis! He was alive, but had lost over half his bodyweight. Apparently, the Honers' four-year-old son Tyce had put the cat in there "to keep him safe" and then forgotten about him. Poor cold kitty!

UNBELIEVABLE!

Whine wedding

Louise Harris, owner of Diva Dogs in Essex, England, loves her pet Lola so much that she spent over $32,000 on a wedding for the pooch.

INCREDIBLE!

Snakes in a car

You've heard of snakes on a plane... well, snakes in a car can cause problems, too. A man in Hartford, Connecticut, crashed his car in 2009 because his two pet snakes crawled under the control pedals. The snakes, both babies, were in his pants pocket, but went wandering and caused the accident when the driver and his passenger tried to catch them.

CRAZY!

Adopted bunny

A baby rabbit was adopted and looked after by a cat named Lucky, owned by Jennifer Anderson of London, Ohio.

A pet cat at an alligator park in Louisiana frightened off a gator by giving it a smack on the snout with its paw!

AMAZING!

A doctor took his pet crocodile for a check-up at a hospital in Croatia! He and his four-foot-long reptile held up the line for hours at the ultrasound department.

Fetch!

Lauren Miller's dog Auggie loved to fetch, like any dog, but could also do ball tricks. He managed to fit five tennis balls into his mouth at once!

Rodent resuscitation

Is this a Christmas miracle? For Christmas the hamster, that is. He was nearly cooked alive when his cage was left on a stove that was accidentally turned on. Firefighters arrived to find him on his back with his legs in the air and his tongue hanging out. They managed to bring him around with oxygen, a few sips of juice, and a gentle tummy rub.

WOW!

Getting stuck

A poor feral cat had its head stuck in a peanut-butter jar for over two weeks before it was rescued by the Cain family of Bartlett, Tennessee.

Superstar

Moonie, the dog from the movie *Legally Blonde*, is paid $1,500 for movie appearances.

AWESOME!

RIPLEY's
EXPENSIVE TASTES

1 In 2007 Pepper the dog was truly in the doghouse.

2 The day before, he had used the contents of his owner's mom's purse as doggie chews—$750!

3 Pepper's poop gave the game away! His owners eventually recovered $647 in soiled notes...

4 ...which they swapped for cleaner cash at the bank.

TALL AND SMALL

Gibson, a Great Dane, is surely one of the world's tallest dogs. In 2006, at age three, he was an incredible

7 FEET 2 INCHES

tall if he stood on his back legs. Gibson, owned by Sandy Hall of Sacramento, California, is an amazing sight on his own, but looks even more striking when he's with his best doggy-pal, Zoie the Chihuahua, who is only 7 inches high!

HEN PARTY

When Renee Biwer married Terry Morris in August 2006, she had an unusual bridesmaid: Henrietta the hen! The clucky lady had been the groom's favorite pet for 12 years, so she couldn't miss the big occasion. Both bride and groom got married on horseback, and Henrietta wore a beautiful outfit of feathers—of course!

WORLD'S UGLIEST DOG

Sam, a Chinese crested dog, was a world champion, but it's not necessarily a title he wanted. The 14-year-old was famous for his unusual face, and for three years in a row he took the title of World's Ugliest Dog. He was certainly no oil painting, with pale eyes, a withered neck, wrinkles, virtually no hair, and a face only his mother could love.

SQUIRREL SKI-SHOW

Twiggy is a squirrel with a talent: She can waterski!
She was rescued by Chuck and Lou Ann Best after
falling out of her nest as a baby. The Bests taught
her to waterski, towed behind a remote-controlled
toy boat, giving her a treat each time she lapped
the pool. Now Twiggy has other rescue-squirrels
as friends, and the troupe perform
at boatshows and on TV.

On the right track

A lost Labrador called Archie managed to reunite himself with his owner by catching the train to his hometown in Scotland. The pair got separated at the station, so Archie hopped on the Aberdeen to Inverness train, and got off 12 minutes later at the correct stop!

Think your cat looks underdressed? There's a Japanese web site to solve that: It sells cat collars and hats to turn your cat into a bunny, frog, leopard, or even characters from books!

CATS ON CAMERA

Ever wondered what your cat does when he's away from home? Jürgen Perthold from Anderson, South Carolina, fitted his tomcat, Mr. Lee, with a special "CatCam" on his collar so he could see what his feline friend was up to during the day.

Ooh, naughty Mr. Lee spying on a bird.

The mini-camera takes a picture every minute to show exactly where the cat goes, what it does, and who it sees.

Back home!

Meeting friends.

Meeting grumpy friends.

Mr. Lee's adventures have been recorded for posterity, and have found fame on the Internet, too.

Wow, the kitty next door.

An unexpected snake in the forest.

FAT CAT

Pets who overeat have weight problems, just like humans. So, the U.K. organization the PDSA (People's Dispensary for Sick Animals) has started a fat-fighting club. One member, Socrates the cat, weighs a massive 22 pounds—the same as a one-year-old human—largely thanks to his love of potato chips.

After his wife died, a man in Beijing, China, decided to keep cockroaches for company, and bred around 200,000 of the creepy-crawly chums.

Sticky situation

Let this be a lesson to dogs who like to chew: Choose your chews carefully. Toby, a Jack Russell terrier from Hampshire, England, mashed his mistress's mail so much that the paper and envelope glue set like papier maché, and stuck the little scamp's jaws together.

LET ME IN

Pet doors can be a great invention, unless yours is a gateway to unwanted wildlife coming into your house. You could try the Pet-2-Ring Doorbell, a clever invention that allows your pet to ring its own doorbell and ask to be let in. Owners are given a video showing how to train their pet to push a lever that rings chimes indoors— no more unwanted guests!

PAMPERED PETS

Make me another
Until 2006, cat lovers with $50,000 to spare could have their beloved pets cloned (another identical version of their cat) by a California company called Genetic Savings & Clone.

INCREDIBLE!

Too many toes
Alison Thomas's cat Des has eight more toes than a normal cat! Most have five on their front paws and four on the back paws, but Des, from Swansea, Wales, has two extra on each foot.

Hot dogs
Dogs in Tokyo, Japan, can take a dip in their very own

WOW!

hot tub! *Onsen* (hot springs) are popular for humans, but now their pet pooches can take a dip for around $25. The doggy tub is filled with volcanic waters at just the right temperature, and afterward the pampered pets can relax in a separate dog-nap room.

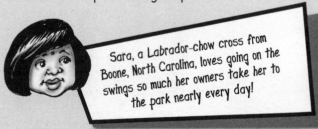

Sara, a Labrador-chow cross from Boone, North Carolina, loves going on the swings so much her owners take her to the park nearly every day!

Fishing cat

Think cats hate water? Think again: The *Felis viverrina* or fishing cat from India has webbed paws, waterproof fur, and dives into the water to catch fish.

In the 1930s, dogs employed as extras in Hollywood films were paid $7.50 a day: the same amount as people!

NO WAY!

Ground dog days

Way back in 1896, a veterinarian named Dr. Samuel Johnson offered to let a friend bury his dog in the apple orchard of his home. Now the plot, in Hartsdale, New York, is a fully fledged pet cemetery with 70,000 beloved bodies buried there.

Precious poop

Dilubhai Rajput, an Indian diamond merchant, had to sort through piles of cow poop to get back 1,722 diamonds that a cow had eaten!

Dating for dogs

The U.K. has its own lonely hearts website for dogs. Owners can log on to find a mate for their mutt, or simply to get health advice for their pets.

SUPERB!

PET PYTHON

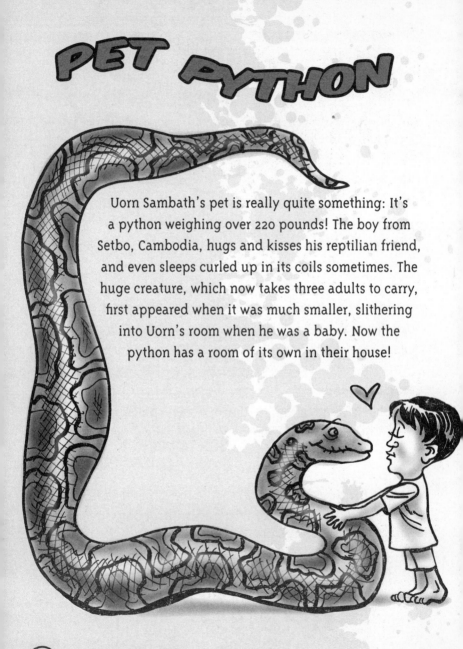

Uorn Sambath's pet is really quite something: It's a python weighing over 220 pounds! The boy from Setbo, Cambodia, hugs and kisses his reptilian friend, and even sleeps curled up in its coils sometimes. The huge creature, which now takes three adults to carry, first appeared when it was much smaller, slithering into Uorn's room when he was a baby. Now the python has a room of its own in their house!

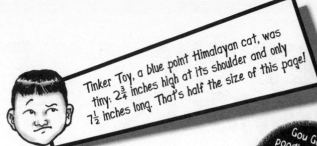

Tinker Toy, a blue point Himalayan cat, was tiny: 2¾ inches high at its shoulder and only 7½ inches long. That's half the size of this page!

Gou Gou the poodle, from Xi'an City, China, goes for a walk every day—hand in hand with her owner, Wang Guoqiang.

Buried alive

A springer spaniel named Lulu was rescued in April 2008 after spending eight days buried under a building. The two-story business block in Breckenridge, Colorado, had exploded, leaving Lulu stranded beneath

15 FEET OF RUBBLE

for over a week. Rescuers heard her whimpering and managed to dig her out. She had survived on melted snow and scraps of food.

PET PIN NUMBERS

Canine Partners is a U.K.-based organization that provides trained dogs to care for people in the most practical ways. The live-in canine carers can help people with physical disabilities by undressing them, unloading the washing machine, opening cupboards, and even taking out money from the A.T.M. at the bank.

The Gagen family's pet cat adopted two baby chicks and raised them at their home in Schenectady, New York.

Two pints, please...

One for Peter Dolan, and one for his horse, Peggy! Peter used to tie up his horse outside while he popped into the pub for a drink at the Alexandra Hotel in Jarrow, England. Peggy followed him indoors one day, and now she's a regular at the bar.

03

B
~~P~~arking ticket

Marilyn Feneley couldn't help but laugh when she collected her faithful dog Curly and found he'd been given a parking ticket! She tied him up, as always, outside her local store in Darwin, Australia, but five minutes later she found a warning notice taped to his leash. According to the authorities, it was an offense to leave the dog unattended in a public place.

Geronimo, a lop-eared rabbit belonging to the Nipper family in Bakersfield, California, has ears that are four times longer than this page!

Pet in the post

A mailman from Cambridge was astonished to collect a package containing

A HAMSTER!

Robert Maher was emptying a mailbox, and found the rodent peeping from an envelope marked "Do not bend." The hamster, nicknamed First Class, was examined by a veterinarian who thought it was lucky to be alive after its passage through the postal sorting system!

NEARLY A CAT-ASTROPHE

Poor Kimba the kitty was squeaky clean after an accident at its home in Sydney, Australia.

The four-month-old kitten took a cat nap in the laundry basket, but ended up taking a spin...

...in the washing machine! Its owner didn't realize that Kimba was in there, until the cycle finished and he opened the door to find...

...a frightened, washed-up pet. Kimba had sore eyes and hypothermia from the cold cycle, but no lasting damage.

RIPLEY'S
DID YOU KNOW???

In 2007, a dog near Jianyang City, China, gave birth to a puppy that looked like a kitten! It had a gene mutation that changed its looks, though it still yapped instead of meowing.

Mrs. Zhang from China owns a dog that yaps and howls to the tune of her ringtone every time she gets a phone call.

Mushu, a pet bearded dragon in Jacksonville, Florida, had to be treated by a veterinarian in 2007 after swallowing a toy lizard that looked too tempting to resist.

A police dog appeared in court in Pittsburgh, Pennsylvania, in 1994. The defense called him to the stand, trying to prove the dog, not the human client, was guilty of fighting.

Judith Dodsworth's pet greyhound, Pikelet, loves to sing opera. Judith is herself an opera singer, and when she starts to sing, so does her dog—very loudly!

J.D. Wilton of Australia trained his horse, Tim, to do amazing tricks. Tim could balance on a single small wooden block with his rider twirling a lasso on his back!